Broken Rib

When a Marriage
Becomes Sick

Broken Rib

When a Marriage Becomes Sick

A religious guide to self-healing your marriage by

Sherri Thomas

**Published by BlackGold Publishing, LLC in partnership with
The BlackGold Book League of Hampton Roads.**

1706 Todds Lane, Suite 258
Hampton, VA 23666

Edited by: Jamel H, Noelle B
Formatted by: Jamel H
First Edition: April 2024
Printed in the United States of America

Acknowledgements

To my heavenly Father, without whom I would not have my being, I am eternally **grateful**. Thank you, Father, for always being present. You are truly the Way, the Truth, and the Life. I am humbled by your Majesty and Power. I am blessed by your Grace and Mercy, which are new every day. Your Holy Spirit is my Comforter and Guide. You light my path, Father, guiding me into destiny and purpose. Thank you, Father, for your Son, Christ Jesus, without whom I would not have the right to approach you and your Holiness. You have given me the blessing of the Ultimate Sacrifice. Your Word is quick and sharper than any two-edged sword. It divides asunder the soul from the spirit and weighs the intents of the heart. Thank you, Father, for you are Holy and Righteous. Thank you for teaching me, my loving Father. Without you, I would not be able to be transformed into who you Will me to be. Thank you, Blessed Father, for covering me and engrafting me into your Kingdom.

To my husband, Daryl, time has afforded us to grow. The twists and turns have not been easy by any standard. Through this journey, we learn how to walk through the fire together. With God on our side, we have grown and cultivated what is uniquely our union. Through God, we are joined. Through God, we are sustained. Through God, we are more than conquerors.

To my loving daughter, Nakiria, thank you, baby, for being uniquely you. You are the fruit of your father and my union. We are indeed blessed. I am proud of you. I love you to life, always. Thank you for your support and care.

To my mother and father, you always taught me that there is greatness within. You always taught me to look to God in all things. Thank you for the foundation you laid. I have had to draw upon the Well that is in Christ Jesus. You taught me to trust Him. Because of this, I never have to thirst. Mom, as I finalize the first two books in this series, you have passed on to Glory. You are forever in my heart. You and Dad were married fifty-eight years at your passing. As I watched Dad standing before you to say his final goodbyes, I learned yet another lesson from you two;

[4] *Love is **patient**, love is **kind**. It does not envy, it does not boast, it is not proud. [5] It does not*

*dishonor others, it is **not self-seeking**, it is not easily angered, it keeps no record of wrongs. ⁶ **Love does not delight in evil** but rejoices with the truth. ⁷ It always protects, always trusts, always hopes, **always perseveres.***

(I Corinthians 13:4-7 NIV)

And to the voice of Wisdom that constantly speaks Life to me, Thank you.

BROKENNESS

By: Sherri Thomas

Lies, Cheating, Deceit
Lord, deliver me from
This rage, churning within me!
Attempting to break the essence

That is me

I refuse to allow Brokenness to
Be the word that defines me

Bitterness, rejection, betrayal
Ingredients of the cake that with
Your actions you chose to have
And will therefore eat too
I refuse to allow myself to be

Lost in you

I am the daughter of the King
You disrespected that with this fling
Thinking you will leave me
In a broken mess
The devil fooled you cause
I'm of a peculiar breed
And nothing less

Five, Six, Seven, Eight
Nine, Ten times you proved
You out here acting like a fool
Over and over again I see
The lies you're trying to tell me

I **AM** the posterity
Of His Royal blood line
Yeah, Straight from above
Fathered by Him only
The Divine
It is you who failed to realize that
I am one of a kind

The devil lied to you
When he tried to use
You as a tool
To erect a monument of
What he thought would
Be my demise
A mirage of brokenness
Meant to bury me in loneliness and
Messages of despair
But he failed to tell you that
My God is ALWAYS,
ALWAYS there
And He truly cares

A wonder in my soul
My Lord, My Savior
My Father, the Great I AM
All that I need is within Him
And He is in me
Every shattered piece
Of me, you left

I gathered and placed upon
The Potter's Wheel
And here I stand completely healed
Born again and genuinely new

Broken,

Broken free
From the prison that is you

Broken? No! No longer broken
But conquering what
Would have been my defeat
I'm praising and honoring
My God who covers me

Blessed be God my Rock
My Strong Tower and Deliverer
I've been broken into pieces
And left to die but God is
My Help that comes from on High
Yes, I've been broken into pieces

But behold I am now:

A mosaic reflection, a testimony
That though you left me in brokenness
I've been forged in the fire that seals me in
Wholeness!

I am no longer
Broken.

Table of Contents

Acknowledgments
"Brokenness" by Sherri Thomas

Introduction

hat does it mean to be "**broken**"?

Merriam Webster offers a variety of definitions, such as "being violently separated into parts" like a shattered glass. "Broken" refers to being damaged or in a weakened state. It represents a state of disconnection, such as in a divorce or marital separation. Often, a marriage is already broken well before the couple acknowledges its fragmented condition. Lines of division were drawn long before the divorce or separation became official. When a marriage becomes broken, the family unit shatters. Discontentment, mistrust, deceit, infidelity, lies, lack of communication, and disrespect wrap around the marriage, threatening to silence its voice. These elements strangle its ability to thrive and survive. Blaming fingers launch daggers of death, killing the life that sustains the marriage. A broken marriage occurs when a death blow is dealt to the covenant that once bound the couple as one.

"Broken Rib: When a Marriage Becomes Sick" aims to address the issue of brokenness that causes dysfunction and discord within the family unit. Brokenness within a marriage leaves the marriage bed cold and hauntingly lonely, resulting in a house that fails to feel like a home. This book offers a soothing balm to inspire healing in that place—the broken rib. Its purpose is to foster dialogue and bring healing rather than discord. Through its pages, may revelation flow into the wounded areas, restoring what has been broken and bestowing wholeness upon the incomplete. May it empower both spouses to live beyond the brokenness.

In God's Service,

Sherri Thomas

Chapter One
Nakedness

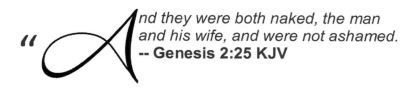

" nd they were both naked, the man and his wife, and were not ashamed.
-- Genesis 2:25 KJV

When was the last time you experienced genuine nakedness in your marriage? I'm referring to the kind where you and your spouse lay bare before each other, unashamed of your transparency. Yes, I mean the kind where you and your spouse expose every flaw and imperfection, completely vulnerable.

Are you secure enough to truly introspect? Where is that level of intimacy in your marriage? Has it ever existed, or has it faded away? If asking that question stirred uneasiness within you, it indicates a guardedness that acts as a barrier to deeper connection with your spouse. It communicates, "I don't trust you to come too close. Keep your distance!" This spirit fosters division and contributes to brokenness in the home. Operating in this manner hinders repair and long-term healing.

Many relationships lack transparency and instead suffocate under deception and mistrust. Neither party is willing to genuinely be themselves. In hindsight, numerous relationships begin with subtle deception. When preparing for a first date, it's common for both individuals to "wear a mask" in hopes of impressing their potential love interest. As the relationship progresses, hidden aspects gradually surface, often shocking the relationship to the point of dissolution or collapse. Remaining true to your authentic self and refusing to compromise who you are is crucial when becoming joined with your spouse.

Key Words:

transparency, trust, vulnerability, nakedness, intimacy, barriers.

Reflection Questions:

1. Explain how transparency looks within your marriage?

_____

_____

_____

_____

_____

_____

2. Is there a fear of being transparent within your marriage? If so, what barriers contribute to your reservation to be transparent with your spouse?

_____

_____

_____

_____

_____

_____

3. How do you and your spouse exhibit trust within your marriage? Is there a fear of being vulnerable with your spouse? Is there a reservation to be spiritually and physically naked with your spouse? Explain.

_____

_____

_____

_____

_____

_____

Healing the Break:

- Reflect upon your responses above. What conclusions can you draw that there may or may not be evidence that your marriage suffers from a lack of intimacy and transparency?

_____

_____

_____

_____

_____

_____

_____

_____

_____

_____

_____

_____

_____

- Is there evidence that there may be a fracture to the rib of your marriage? If so, list three things

you are willing to do to minister to this area of
need within your marriage.

_____

_____

_____

_____

_____

_____

_____

_____

_____

_____

_____

_____

_____

- Reserve some time to sit with your spouse to agree upon three things you both need to do to minister to this area of need. Invest time to address those areas of needs. Note how these things have improved your marriage and what needs more work. Communicate with your spouse to work toward improvement.

_____

_____

_____

_____

_____

_____

_____

_____

_____

_____

_____

_____

_____

_____

- Seek professional help such as your Pastor and/or marriage counselor to help guide you through this process.

Prayer

Father, *dispel the darkness of deceit, hidden agendas, and secrecy that hoover over my marriage. Allow your Spirit to flow into my marriage to shine a light upon what makes it sick. Restore trust in my marriage, Father. Construct more effective lines of communication between my husband/wife and I. Remove the barriers that blockade the ability of my marriage to grow vibrantly. Father, help my husband/wife and I to be transparent with one another. Bless my husband/wife and I as we seal our interactions with the intimacy of truth and no ill-will toward one another. Bless our home, dear Father. We honor you and acknowledge you as you direct us in how to have "authentic nakedness" within our marriage. Through the precious blood of the Lamb I pray. Thank you, Father. Amen.*

Chapter Two
Who Am I To You

"*And Adam said, This is now bone of my bones, and flesh of my flesh; she shall be called woman, because she was taken out of man...*
-- Genesis 2:23 KJV

Frequently, individuals enter marriage only to realize they've lost themselves in the process, leading to confusion about their identity. When Adam beheld Eve standing before him, he exclaimed, "This is now bone of my bones, and flesh of my flesh." Although God presented her to him, it was Adam who had to discern their connection. Eve wasn't merely an object of physical desire or subservience to Adam's needs or ego. When Adam gazed upon Eve, he recognized and declared who she was to him – "bone of my bones, and flesh of my flesh." He saw Eve for who she truly was, acknowledging their profound connection; nothing else in the garden could match their level of companionship and growth.

How often do we truly perceive the depth of our connection with our spouse? The challenge in many relationships lies in the ambiguity surrounding each other's roles; one partner may view the relationship casually, while the other perceives it as a committed bond. Genesis 2:18 emphasizes the importance of companionship. Adam, spiritually bonded with God, sought a companion to share that bond. Are you depleting your true essence by investing in a relationship solely focused on physical aspects?

It's crucial for spouses to possess the spiritual maturity to discern beyond each other's physical attributes and understand the deeper qualities planted by God. Additionally, do you and your spouse understand what draws you into union with each other? Ladies, do you comprehend how your "Adam" perceives you? Gentlemen, do you grasp what your "Eve" sees as she stands before you? Ultimately, do you and your spouse recognize the profound connectedness that unites you as one? Indeed, marital partners should have insight into each other and celebrate the inherent beauty and strength bestowed upon them by God. They should understand what qualifies them to stand beside each other and never undermine the uniqueness that defines their essence.

Traditional teachings often portray Adam as alone and in need of a helper. Furthermore, some may argue that Adam required a woman to fulfill his needs as a man, relegating her to the role of a weaker vessel responsible solely for procreation. This perspective fosters gender conflicts and detracts from the essential unity of Adam and Eve. Such misconceptions have infiltrated many marriages, resulting in one-dimensional relationships lacking balance and growth.

Adam, as the only being in creation lacking

balance, required someone equal to walk beside him. Therefore, a fundamental aspect of marriage is recognizing who your spouse is to you. How do you define your spouse in your life? What role do they play? If it relegates them to walking behind or beneath you, it builds a faulty foundation that suppresses the greatness and essence of the one placed in such a position.

In retrospect, marriage is a covenant of respect and honor. Eve was taken from Adam's side, symbolizing her position. For her to walk with Adam, her position must originate from his side. Respect and honor are crucial components that sustain marriage. Once Eve was taken from Adam's side and God sealed the place from which she was taken, He presented her to Adam so he could recognize her role in his life. Although Adam was asleep when God created Eve from his side, he inherently knew her—she had been protecting his heart. God fashioned Eve and then revealed her to Adam, allowing him to see what had been within him, supporting him before he was even aware of it.

Without this understanding of Eve's identity, her position in relation to Adam would have been lost in the overgrowth of the garden they were meant to cultivate together. Additionally, Eve would have been uncertain about how Adam perceived her in relation to him. She would have been present but unable to fulfill her role as a "help meet." Consequently, many individuals date for years without committing due to the lack of genuine clarity in their relationships. Instead, they orbit the concept of covenant without fully embracing it.

12

Adam, be cautious in how you perceive Eve—she resided within you, guarding your most vital parts while you slumbered, preparing to meet her. How do you recognize Eve? She is intimately and deeply connected to you, known to you at sight. Eve, ensure you understand your identity before approaching Adam. Although you were within him before he laid eyes on you, comprehend who you are so you can effectively stand beside him.

Key Words:

self-awareness, security, connection, position, intimacy

Reflection Questions:

1. On a scale of 1-10, how would you rate the intimacy level in your marriage, considering the physical, spiritual, and emotional perspectives?

_____

_____

_____

_____

_____

_____

2. Why do you believe Adam and Eve embraced transparency, trust, vulnerability, nakedness, and intimacy within their marriage in the Garden of Eden?

_____

_____

_____

_____

_____

3. How do you and your spouse connect with each other, both on a day-to-day basis and in deeper, meaningful ways?

_____

_____

_____

_____

_____

Healing the Break:

- Reflect on moments in your marriage when the connection with your spouse is most evident. (These moments could include shared experiences, emotional support, understanding, and mutual growth.)

_____

_____

_____

_____

_____

_____

_____

_____

_____

_____

_____

_____

_____

_____

- Identify one specific way you will commit to nurturing and strengthening the connection you have with your spouse. (This could involve improving communication, spending quality time together, showing appreciation and affection, or addressing any areas of tension or misunderstanding.)

_____

_____

_____

_____

_____

_____

_____

_____

_____

_____

_____

Prayer

Father, *help me to have self-awareness. Strengthen me, O' Lord, that I may be who you designated me to be. Father, help my marriage to be secure. Anoint the connection between my husband/wife and I. Father, secure my position in my marriage. Abundantly bless the intimacy that my husband/wife and I share. Keep my husband/wife and I connected and strong. Fill my husband/wife with your Spirit, O' Lord. Help us to be sure and confident in who we are to each other. Keep my husband/wife and I connected and strong. Through the power of Your Holy Spirit, I will manifest healthy and wholesome communication and expression as I relate to my husband/wife. Through the power of Your Holy Spirit we will establish a stable and secure foundation for our marriage. Through the blood of the Lamb I pray and honor You. Amen.*

Chapter Three

What Is Your Place

"*And the lord God caused a deep sleep to fall upon Adam and he slept; and he took one of his ribs and closed up the flesh thereof; 22) And the rib, which the Lord God had taken from man made he a woman and brought her unto the man*-- **Genesis 2:21-22 KJV**

"*Stay in your place, woman!*" How often has this been said? What is Eve's place? Based on scripture, we know that she came from Adam's side. She was pulled from the inside of him, and God built her. In this respect, Eve's place is sacred, not to be viewed as a position of weakness or convenience. In retrospect, the place from which Eve was taken is so sacred that God had to close it so that no one else could imitate her. Her position was solidified in that distinct moment when God sealed that place.

Therefore, respect and honor sealed her position. Her place is not to be taken lightly. When Adam looked at Eve, he recognized her role in his life. She is woman; that part of him that carries a womb. She nurtures and gives birth. She has the capacity to help Adam be "fruitful and multiply." She is capable of going through the labor required to birth vision. She knows how to travail and deliver. Yes, when Adam looked at Eve, he recognized whom he was looking at. There was no doubt about her place. Yes, Eve's place was beside him. When Eve stood before Adam, she did not reject him. She joined him in the Garden. She showed him respect and honor. Together, that is how they would walk through the garden, utilizing the authority that God gave them both. Respecting that will prohibit ego and a spirit of dominance from handicapping that walk. Respect will allow the two to walk together in unison without forgetting the special place the other has in their life. Know who you are in your marriage; that distinction must be clear. Marriage must have clarity. If there is uncertainty and confusion concerning the position of your spouse in your life, then the marriage will die. Moreover, mistrust and discord will plague the marriage. Your spouse's position is beside you. This regards every facet of the relationship. No one or nothing should transpose that position.

Key Words:

sight, position, honor, trust

Reflection Questions:

1. How do you see your spouse? How does your spouse see you?

_____

_____

_____

2. What is your position regarding how you walk with your spouse? Is there evidence of power play between you and your spouse? Explain.

_____

_____

_____

_____

_____

_____

3. What evidence is there of honor and trust in your marriage?

_____

_____

_____

_____

_____

_____

Healing the Break:

- Discuss and actively engage in ways that you and your spouse will focus on honoring and trusting one another.

- List those ways and discuss your progress below.

_____

_____

_____

_____

_____

_____

_____

_____

_____

Prayer

Father, *give me spiritual sight in my marriage. Help me, Father, to see my husband/wife and their position to me. O'Lord help me to honor and trust my husband/wife. I look to you, Father, to guide me in my marriage. Help me, Father, to see clearly that I need to heal fractures that lie between my husband/wife and I. Through the blood of the Lamb I pray. I acknowledge you as you direct me. Thank you, Father. Amen.*

Chapter Four

Who's Speaking

"*Now the serpent was more crafty than any of the wild animals the Lord God had made. He said to the woman, "Did God really say, you must not eat from any tree in the garden?".*
-- Genesis 3:1 NIV

How often have we allowed other people and things to attack, threaten, or even usurp the place that rightfully belongs to our spouse? This question is for both the man and the woman in a marital relationship. Has the place from which your rib was taken been sealed? Is it protected? Has someone else been allowed to rest in that place? Allowing others to make themselves at home in the space that your spouse is supposed to occupy will result in a systematic breakdown in the marital organs.

The snake spoke louder into Adam and Eve's marriage than he should have been allowed. Have you allowed someone's voice from the outside to impose itself upon the communication that should be between you and your spouse? To whom have you been listening? Does that voice reverberate more intensely and have more impact on the outcome of what should be agreed upon between you and your spouse? Quite frankly, are you allowing someone or something outside of your marital union to have control over your marriage? Is it controlling your home? Why are those voices so comfortable in your marriage?

If you said yes to any of these questions, then your marriage has a **broken rib.** It is sick. If attention is not given to this emergency, then it will not survive. What are the voices, opinions, and imposing perspectives that have been allowed to force themselves into your union? Please know that these voices can come from anywhere or from any source. Allowing these voices to press upon your marriage may kill it. Ignoring what or who has been given power to control your marriage will result in you wandering alone in the garden of your marriage. So, who's speaking in your marriage?

Key Words:

communication, imposition, perspective, voice, relationship, boundaries

Reflection Questions:
1. Explain how you and your spouse communicate with one another. Is there evidence that communication between you and your spouse is effective or ineffective? Explain.

24

_____

_____

_____

_____

_____

_____

2. How well do you hear and understand the voice of your spouse? Explain. Are imposing perspectives allowed to interfere with the communication between you and your spouse? Explain.

_____

_____

_____

_____

_____

_____

3. What voices are you listening to regarding your marriage? Are outside opinions allowed to impose upon your marriage? Explain.

_____

_____

_____

_____

_____

_____

4. What boundaries are set to ensure that the perspective of your spouse is not overshadowed by imposing perspectives from outside of your marriage?

_____

_____

_____

_____

_____

_____

Healing the Break:

- Schedule a heart-to-heart discussion with your spouse. Ask them if there have been instances where they felt unheard or their voice was not valued in your marriage. Listen attentively without interruptions, allowing them to express their feelings openly. Consider engaging in a brief free-writing exercise individually to reflect on moments when you perceived your spouse giving more weight to outside perspectives over yours. Share your feelings and articulate your expectations for better mutual respect in the future.

- Monitor and acknowledge the progress made in addressing communication issues within your marriage (Record it below). Commit to actively safeguarding and enhancing communication channels moving forward.

_____

_____

_____

_____

_____

_____

_____

_____

_____

_____

_____

_____

_____

Prayer

*Help me, **Father**. Establish your hedge of protection around my marriage. Be the fortress for my marriage, Father, that no one and nothing may penetrate its sustainability. Guide my husband/wife and I as we communicate. Help us to see the Divine perspective in all our marital matters. Open our ears, Father to hear your voice and to refrain from being distracted by destructive influences. Bless the union between my husband/wife and I. Guard us against imposing forces that seek to destroy our marriage. Through the blood of the Lamb we pray. We acknowledge you as you guide us in Truth. We open ourselves to you, Father that you may flow through us, our marriage, and our home. Amen.*

Chapter Five

Snake In The Garden

Split by The Tip of the Serpent's Tongue

"*Now the serpent was more crafty than any of the wild animals the Lord God had made. He said to the woman, "Did God really say, "You must not eat from any tree in the garden?"*
-- Genesis 3:1 NIV

All who are married must realize that within the blissful union lies a serpent! Despite how fortified one may feel, a serpent slithers around the garden, awaiting the opportunity to speak into your ear. It lurks, wrapping itself around the fruit of every promise, waiting to strike! It lusts after the confidence and security in your relationship with God, seeking to distract and inject venom into your life. The serpent, envious and hateful, lies camouflaged in the garden, hissing lies with the intent to kill, steal, and destroy what God has established.

This serpent strategically aims for Adam's side, targeting the rib to fracture and break it beyond repair. Its venom spreads to the heart of the vision and destiny ordained by God for the relationship between mankind and Himself. Cunningly watching, the serpent contemplates schemes to break Adam's rib, lurking in the shadows of the garden.

Reflect on the serpent in your own garden, envious of your relationship with God and your spouse. It skulks, waiting to distort messages between you and God, weaving a blanket of darkness over your sacred union. Beware its forked tongue, poised to pierce the fabric of your life, weaving chaos and instability into your marriage.

Don't let the serpent sneak upon you, for it can bite your marriage, causing sickness and, in some cases, fatal division. Many marriages are indeed split by the lies flowing from the serpent's tongue.

Key Words:

mixed messages, lies, deceit, division, venomous words

Reflection Questions:

1. What conflicting messages have been conveyed in your marriage?

_____

_____

_____

_____

_____

_____

2. What hurtful words, lies, or deceitful messages have been spoken into your marriage, causing division between you and your spouse?

_____

_____

_____

_____

_____

3. Where have these messages originated? Identify their source and how they managed to infiltrate your marriage.

_____

_____

_____

_____

_____

_____

Healing the Break:

- Set aside time with your spouse to contemplate the questions above, aiming for growth and healing in your relationship.
- Listen to your spouse's heart with love and respect, committing to muting the sources of these damaging messages and focusing on healing the divisions they have caused.

- Monitor and acknowledge the progress made together, sharing updates with your spouse. Share one below.

_____

_____

_____

_____

_____

Prayer

*Lord **God**, there are snakes in my garden. Jehovah kill the mixed messages that poison my marriage. Father, inject the serum of your Holy Word to make my husband/wife and I immune to the venomous lies and deceit that create division between us. Lord God, heal the wounds inflicted by lies that have bitten our marriage. Lord God, heal those areas of our marriage that fester from the venom of every toxic word of mixed messages. Lord God, we open our hearts and all our being to you. We look to you as the authority in our lives and our marriage, Lord. Help my marriage, Father from these deadly bites from the enemy. We look to you Father. We honor you, Father. We acknowledge you as you guide us in healing and Truth. Through the precious blood of the Lamb we pray. Amen.*

Chapter Six

Snake Bite

"Now the serpent was more crafty than any of the wild animals the Lord God had made. He said to the woman, "Did God really say, "You must not eat from any tree in the garden?" 2) The woman said to the serpent, "We may eat fruit from the trees in the garden, but God did say, "You must not eat fruit from the tree that is in the middle of the garden, and you must not touch it, or you will die." 4) You will not certainly die, "the serpent said to the woman. 5) For God knows that when you eat from it your eyes will be opened, and you will be like God, knowing good and evil." 6) When the woman saw that the fruit of the tree was good for food and pleasing to the eye, and also desirable for gaining wisdom, she took some and ate it. She also gave some to her husband, who was with her, and he ate it. 7) Then the eyes of both of them were opened, and they realized they were naked; so they sewed fig leaves together and made coverings for themselves. **-- Genesis 3:1-7 NIV**

As a woman who grew up in the countryside, I am well acquainted with the dangers posed by snakes. "Beware of snakes!" is a familiar warning from parents whose homes are nestled in the embrace of nature's arms. The threat of being bitten by these venomous creatures is enough to keep any rural resident on high alert. It's not uncommon to step outside and find oneself face-to-face with these deadly reptiles. I vividly remember a few instances from my carefree childhood when I ventured out to play in the warm sunshine, only to realize, upon closer inspection, that I had narrowly avoided stepping on a viperous serpent. With just a few more steps, it could have easily struck me, leaving me to cry out for help and scramble to counteract the effects of its venomous bite.

Deception is the cunningly hypnotic tool Satan employs to sow doubt in our minds about what we know to be true. He slithers toward his intended victim, opening his mouth and flicking his forked tongue. The serpent's tongue, how seductive are the words that flow from it! It taps into the deepest secrets buried within our souls. How often have we been ensnared, believing we had escaped its grasp? The serpent's tongue is adept at creating the division that plagues many marriages worldwide. It may appear united until its tip, but, in reality, couples often find themselves divided, much like the serpent's tongue. Hidden emotions and unspoken truths fester until the marriage is torn asunder.

The serpent bares its sharp fangs, poised to strike. It preys on areas of weakness, knowing this increases its chances of paralyzing its intended victim in preparation for the kill. Has Satan's bite pierced the veins of your marriage? Have lies and deceit been allowed to infiltrate the very heart of what you and your spouse vowed to build together? Take a moment to assess the pulse of your marriage. Are there signs that you've been bitten?

The crafty serpent camouflages itself within the

surroundings, waiting to coil around the neck of your vows. It seeks to look into your eyes and convince you of the truth of its lies, right before it destroys your "*I do*."

Key Words:

deception, persuasion, decisions

Reflection Questions:

1. Recall a moment when you were persuaded to act against what you and your spouse had previously discussed, prayed about, and received God's direction on. Reflect on the impact that decision had on your marriage.

_____

_____

_____

_____

_____

_____

2. After being persuaded to act against what was discussed and agreed upon with your

spouse, explore the feelings of betrayal and division that surfaced. Journal these reflections not to dwell in bitterness but to learn from them thoughtfully.

_____

_____

_____

_____

_____

_____

3. Reflect on a moment in your marriage when the blame game ensued after external deception led to division, similar to Adam and Eve. Consider what you would do differently to better protect your marriage against such outside influences.

_____

_____

_____

_____

_____

_____

Healing the Break:

- Take a moment to quiet your thoughts and reflect on challenging moments where you and your spouse violated your covenant. This includes any breach of fidelity in your relationship. Identify and list these instances below.

- Breathe deeply as you purposefully silence voices of blame, hurt, betrayal, and divisiveness. Simply exhale a confession of "I'm sorry" or "I was wrong." Specifically list the things for which you are sorry.

_____

_____

_____

_____

_____

_____

_____

_____

_____

_____

_____

- Release the need for blame, shame, or finger-pointing. Remove the "fig leaves" (lies) you've used to cover your mistakes. List these "fig leaves" and describe how you will remove them from your marriage.

_____

_____

_____

_____

_____

_____

_____

_____

_____

_____

_____

- Heal the breach by embracing one another and reaffirming your commitment to protect your covenant. Discuss what is necessary to reconnect and move forward together.

_____

_____

_____

_____

_____

_____

_____

_____

_____

_____

Prayer

Father, *thank you for redemption. Thank you, Father, for being our healer both physically as well as spiritually. Father, you encamp round about us. You have commissioned your ministering angels and warring angels to minister to us and to guard us. Your Word, Oh! Lord, is our shield and buckler. Father, pour Your Word into us. Anoint us with Your Spirit, Father. Anoint us to discern Truth. Empower us to resist the devil and according to your Word if we do that he must flee. Father, our marriage will no longer be poisoned by snake bite. The serum of Your Truth* *heals every wound inflicted upon our marriage. We lift our marriage to You, Father that you may reverse the toxins that course through the veins of our marriage. We declare healing and victory in our marriage this day. We declare that no weapon constructed to bring down our marriage will prosper. We declare every foul lie and deceptive dagger that has penetrated the bounds of our marriage is hereby destroyed and rendered of non-effect. We drink from the cup of your redeeming Power and Authority, Father. We declare that no slithering, cunning, and deceptive serpent will be able to enter the garden of our marriage to inject venom. We walk in the Authority of Your Word. We are no longer the victim of Satan's deception. We are heirs to Your Kingdom; a Royal priesthood and a chosen nation. Our marriage is strengthened and fed through the precious Blood of the Lamb. In the name of Yeshua we pray. We honor You, Father. Thank you, Father. Amen.*

Chapter Seven

Venom:

A Lethal Injection

"*Now the serpent was more crafty than any of the wild animals the Lord God had made. He said to the woman, "Did God really say, "You must not eat from any tree in the garden?" 2) The woman said to the serpent, "We may eat fruit from the trees in the garden, but God did say, "You must not eat fruit from the tree that is in the middle of the garden, and you must not touch it, or you will die." 4) You will not certainly die, "the serpent said to the woman. 5) For God knows that when you eat from it your eyes will be opened, and you will be like God, knowing good and evil." 6) When the woman saw that the fruit of the tree was good for food and pleasing to the eye, and also desirable for gaining wisdom, she took some and ate it. She also gave some to her husband, who was with her, and he ate it. 7) Then the eyes of both of them were opened, and they realized they were naked; so they sewed fig leaves together and made coverings for themselves.*

-- Genesis 3:1-7 NIV

A snake bite is unmistakable, releasing venom—a lethal injection. Snakes are adept at swiftly striking and injecting their poison into their victims, often charming them before the attack. While rattlesnakes may warn with their tail rattles, other snakes silently stalk their prey. In the Garden of Eden, the snake likely didn't give a warning, silently observing Eve's movements and weaknesses. Approaching her confidently when she was alone, he struck. Similarly, in marriages, being physically together doesn't guarantee emotional or spiritual presence.

When a marriage deteriorates to cohabitation without connection, signs of separation become evident. Communication is lost amidst distrust, skepticism, resentment, disappointment, and brokenness. This creates an opening for the snake to enter the crevice of a broken union. The serpent targeted Eve because there was a disconnect between her and Adam. Satan's deception lay in his approach, engaging Eve, convincing her of deprivation, and tempting her to indulge in forbidden fruit. Marital couples, when disconnected, expose themselves to the serpent's approach, leaving needs unattended and vulnerabilities ripe for exploitation. The serpent preys upon uncertainties and doubts when communication falters, easily infiltrating through the crack in the marital rib, whispering marital death into their ears…

14) But each one is tempted when he is dragged away, enticed and baited [to commit sin]by his own [worldly] desire (lust, passion).

-- James 1:14 AMP Bible

The serpent cunningly persuaded Eve that she had been denied too long, convincing her that God was withholding things that could make her happier and greater than Him. He projected onto Eve the same spirit that caused him to be expelled from Heaven, aiming to transfer it to her and ultimately disrupt her relationship with God. By targeting the rib, he sought to move Adam and Eve out of position, destabilizing their relationship. Be cautious of those who try to project onto you the same spirit that caused their downfall, aiming to disrupt your position and stability in your relationship with God and your spouse.

The serpent preys on hidden desires, appealing to dormant or unrealized thoughts. Eve likely pondered the forbidden fruit before, wondering why God prohibited it. When the serpent suggested trying it, it appealed to her contemplations. She allowed her mind to entertain opposing thoughts to God's direction, leading to temptation. The serpent, like a keen sensor, detected Eve's inner thoughts, sensing the frailty in her communication with Adam. He approached her, knowing how to charm her into acting upon those hidden desires she had previously contemplated.

1) Now the serpent was more crafty than any of the wild animals the Lord God had made. He said to the woman, "Did God really say, "You must not eat from any tree in the garden?" 2) The woman said to the serpent, "We may eat fruit from the trees in the garden, but God did say, "You must not eat fruit from the tree that is in the middle of the garden, and you must not touch it, or you will die." 4) You will not certainly die, "the serpent said to the woman. 5) For God knows that when you eat from it your eyes will be opened, and you will be like God, knowing good and evil."

-- Genesis 3: 1-5 NIV

Indeed, the serpent charmed Eve by echoing doubts she already harbored about God's instructions to her and her husband. As God created everything, the serpent observed the care taken to form Adam, noting the intimate connection God had with him. God bent down to the Earth to form Adam and breathed the "breath of life into him," demonstrating a special bond. Satan, observing this, sought to "kill, steal, and destroy" that bond, just as he aimed to usurp God's throne. When he attacks, he targets the God within you, aiming to break the relationship between you and the Lord. In the Garden of Eden, Satan aimed to break Adam and his relationship with God, waiting for the opportunity to strike.

18) {sic} It is not good that the man should be alone; I will make him an help meet for him. 21) And the Lord God caused a deep sleep to fall upon Adam, and he slept: and he took one of his ribs, and closed up the flesh instead thereof; 22) And the rib, which the Lord God had taken from man, made he a woman, and brought her unto the man.

-- Genesis 2: 18, 21-22 NIV

The serpent lay in wait, observing the development of Adam and Eve's union. Under the guise of God's creation, the serpent plotted his attack, eyeing Adam's side as God formed Eve from his rib. The serpent aimed to weaken Adam's side, preventing him from functioning as a complete unit with his intended partner. His plan was to inject poison into their unity, causing division and chaos that would ultimately lead to the demise of their purpose. When the serpent charmed Eve and bit her in the Garden, his venom spread through their family unit, leaving a trail of brokenness evident in every fractured family today. By biting Adam's side and breaking his rib, the serpent aimed to destroy any hope of repair. So, when does it become evident that the rib is indeed broken?

Key Words:

lethal conversation, divisive language, hidden thoughts

Reflection Questions:

1. Reflect on any divisive thoughts you harbor and how they affect your communication with your spouse. Have these thoughts influenced the way you express yourself or interact with your spouse?

_____

_____

_____

_____

_____

_____

2. Recall a recent instance where you allowed outside influences or negative thoughts to create a divide between you and your spouse. Identify the sources of these influences and how they preyed on your vulnerabilities and doubts about your relationship.

_____

_____

_____

_____

_____

3. Consider how you're protecting your mind from engaging in harmful conversations that could potentially harm your marriage. What strategies are you implementing to guard against negative influences?

_____

_____

_____

_____

_____

_____

Healing the Break:

- Take a moment to reflect and review past conversations with your spouse that were unproductive or led to conflict. Write down your reflections on these interactions.

_____

_____

_____

_____

_____

_____

_____

_____

_____

_____

_____

_____

- Document any words or statements you
  made to your spouse that contributed to
  division between you. What were your
  intentions or goals behind these words?

_____

_____

_____

_____

_____

_____

_____

_____

_____

_____

_____

_____

- Release the need for blame, shame, or
  finger-pointing. Remove the "fig leaves"
  (lies) you've used to cover your mistakes.
  List these "fig leaves" and describe how
  you will remove them from your marriage.

_____

_____

_____

_____

_____

_____

_____

_____

_____

_____

_____

- Evaluate whether the words you spoke served to strengthen or weaken the bond between you and your spouse. Reflect on the impact of your communication on your relationship.

- Identify at least three alternative approaches or strategies that could have been used to handle the conversation differently and promote unity with your spouse (list them below). Discuss these with your spouse to understand their perspective and needs in communication and decision-making. Monitor your progress and commit to improving communication in your marriage.

_____

_____

_____

_____

_____

_____

_____

_____

_____

_____

Prayer

Jehovah, *thank you that you are the God of peace. Jehovah still the divisive thoughts that my spouse and I may harbor within our soul. Father, speak to us through your Holy Word. Father, intensify our spiritual discernment that we may be alert to the deceptive approach of "serpents" that encroach upon our marriage. Father, seal the breach that caused my spouse and I to turn away from one another. Jehovah, help us through Your Holy Spirit to hear the heart of one another. Help us, Oh! Lord to not tear each other down. Help us, Father, to build the trust within our marriage that our marriage may be healthy and whole. Help us, Father, to build healthy communication with one another. Help us, Father, that we seek you in every area of our lives. Help us, Father, that we receive the healing Balm that is your Word. Place your Word as a Guard for the gates of our hearing, seeing, tasting, feeling, and even smelling, oh! Lord. Father we adore You and honor You as you protect us from all lethal injections that have already penetrated our marriage. Father, we speak life to every injured area of our marriage. We come to You, Father. Make us whole in the Name of Yeshua, we pray. Thank You, Father. Amen.*

Chapter Eight
Vital Signs:

Adam- You are Hemorrhaging

"*The woman said to the serpent, "We may eat fruit from the trees in the garden, but God did say, "You must not eat fruit from the tree that is in the middle of the garden, and you must not touch it, or you will die." 4) You will not certainly die, "the serpent said to the woman. 5) For God knows that when you eat from it your eyes will be opened, and you will be like God, knowing good and evil."* **-- Genesis 3:2-5 NIV**

Adam and Eve, can't you see that your relationship is fractured, your unity shattered? Can't you feel the distance growing between you, pulling you apart? Eve, do you not realize that Adam is absent from your shared purpose, your joint journey? You are no longer walking hand in hand towards your goals, no longer bearing fruit together as you were intended. Instead, you find yourself engaging with the deceptive whispers of a snake.

Adam, your presence is sorely missed in your home. The serpent, an enemy not just to your marriage but to your very connection with God, has infiltrated your sacred space and is tearing your union apart from within. Your relationship is hemorrhaging, your bond broken. How can you not recognize the insidious force scheming to destroy your marriage? Entertaining the influence of snakes in your marriage invites poison that will corrode its very foundation. Adam, you are bleeding out – a clear sign of marital distress.

When Eve was bitten, she and Adam were not walking in harmony in the Garden. She was alone, a reflection of the breakdown in their relationship. Despite being physically present, they were emotionally and spiritually distant from each other. What changed from the moment Eve was presented to Adam? What caused them to drift apart, to no longer see eye to eye?

You may question, how can we be sure there was trouble in the marriage? Look at the scene. Eve was isolated in the Garden when the serpent charmed her. This signifies emotional, physical, and spiritual discord in their relationship. The serpent seized the opportunity when they were vulnerable and disconnected. Marital breakdown occurs when a couple is no longer united. It stems from unshared conversations, hidden thoughts, and secrets kept from one another. What conversations have you engaged in that you haven't shared with your spouse? Who have you confided in about intimate details of your marriage? Could a snake have infiltrated and poisoned your relationship? Take the time to reflect on where and when your marriage was bitten. Have you neglected to address the issues, allowing the poison to spread? Check the vital signs of your marriage – is it suffering from a broken rib?

The Other Side
By Sherri Thomas

-- Lying in this cold marital bed
Wondering why you
Have turned your back to me
Instead of reaching out to me
You embrace the still coldness of
The silence that lay on the
Other side of what
Does not include me

What do you find there
That you lay determined to
Place it between you and I
A dividing line denying me
Of what is mine

Why don't you turn back
'to me and talk to me
Let us return to what
Is supposed to be
Between you and me
Away from the other side
That draws the dividing line
To keep us away from the
Promise of together
Through all types of weather

Key Words:

unity, marital heartbeat, love

Reflection Questions:

1. Can you feel the heartbeat of your spouse? Describe in your own words what it feels like.

_____

_____

_____

_____

_____

_____

2. Are you and your spouse in harmony with each other's rhythms? Being in sync with your spouse doesn't mean losing your individuality. It's about celebrating your unique selves while also embracing the beautiful harmony you create together. Note down instances where you and your spouse are in sync.

_____

_____

_____

_____

_____

_____

3. Why is it important for you and your
   spouse to understand each other's
   heartbeat? What steps can you take to
   truly listen to your spouse and
   comprehend their needs?

_____

_____

_____

_____

_____

_____

Healing the Break:

- Engage in an open, heartfelt
  conversation with your spouse. Explore
  any unmet needs they may have within
  the marriage.

- Make a commitment to address and heal
  the areas in your marriage that need
  attention the most.

- Take deliberate steps to strengthen areas of vulnerability that cause division in your marriage. List three specific actions you will take to nurture your marriage, and regularly evaluate your progress in these endeavors.

_____

_____

_____

_____

_____

_____

_____

_____

_____

_____

_____

_____

Prayer

Father, thank You for being our God. Father, we come repenting for areas in our marriage where we simply are not being sensitive to the needs of one another. Father, help us to align our heart to Your Word that our desires and needs are in sync with Your Will. Father, we lift our marriage to you for we are broken. Father, help us to hear Your heart that we may beat rhythmically in tune with Your Will for our lives. Father, our marriage is broken, BUT you are our healer… our Redeemer. Father, Your Will be done in our marriage and in our lives. Thank you, for the fresh Breath of Life You are breathing into us and into our marriage. We worship You Oh! Lord. We magnify You above all our issues and our pain. We honor You Oh! Lord. Now we look unto Your Rhema Word as you flow into the crevices of all broken places within us and in our covenant as husband and wife. How wonderful are Your Works Oh! Lord. You are the medicine that cures all sickness and disease. Our marriage will never be the same but whole in the Name of Yeshua we pray. We declare Your Will be done. Thank you. Father. Amen.

Chapter Nine

Roots Of Bitterness

The Blame Game

"*Who told you that you were naked?" the Lord God asked. "Have you eaten from the tree whose fruit I commanded you not to eat?" 12) The man replied, "It was the woman you gave me who gave me the fruit, and I ate it." 13) Then the Lord God asked the woman, "What have you done?" "The serpent deceived me," she replied. "That's why I ate it."* -- **Genesis 3:11-13 NLT**

"The blame game" - How many bitter fruits sprout from those who engage in it? Does the scenario described above resonate with you? How often do we find ourselves exposed, stripped of defenses, by our own mistakes or misguided choices? How many times have seemingly innocent decisions or actions led to unforeseen consequences? When was the last time we allowed ourselves to be persuaded by deceitful whispers, leading us down paths that threaten to unravel the very fabric of our family?

When bitterness takes root, it becomes all too easy to assign blame. Our vision becomes clouded, obscured by resentment. Instead of seeking truth, we embrace tainted narratives of who should bear the fault. The truth is, Eve, Adam, and the serpent all share

61

culpability. Satan's rebellion and disobedience led to his fall from heaven, and he sought to plant the seeds of that same spirit in the Garden of Eden, employing cunning manipulation with Eve. With Adam and Eve out of sync, the serpent found ample space to roam freely in their garden — their home. What ruptured marital bond allowed the serpent to slither into their marriage? What darkness has crept into your own marriage? Is it a lack of communication, commitment, infidelity, lies, or disrespect? What has erected barriers of mistrust between you and your spouse, leading to finger-pointing?

When bitterness takes hold, its symptoms are unmistakable. We no longer see our spouse in the same light. What once drew our admiration — their presence, companionship, and unique qualities — now grates on us. We fail to appreciate the little things we once cherished. Responsibility for the breakdown within the union is shirked, drowned out by a chorus of excuses. Identify where the fracture began, where the roots of bitterness lie. Be candid about what truly causes your discontent with your spouse. Release the bitterness from your spirit, opting instead for healing.

Key Words:

bitterness, betrayal, blame, hidden concerns

Reflection Questions:
1. List the one thing that your spouse has done for which you struggle to forgive them.

_____

_____

_____

_____

_____

_____

2. Do you want your marriage to heal and
   overcome the division from which it suffers?
   Why?

_____

_____

_____

_____

_____

_____

3. What is it you desire from your spouse that
   would open the door of your heart to trust
   him/her again?

_____

_____

_____

_____

_____

_____

Healing The Break:

Reflect upon the following questions. Be *honest.*

1. Are you transparent about your feelings and concerns with your spouse? Do disagreements often escalate into harmful accusations and heated arguments? What holds more significance for you - assigning blame or seeking resolution?

_____

_____

_____

_____

_____

2. Identify the aspects of your marriage that bring you sorrow. Why do these factors hold significance in the context of your marriage?

_____

_____

_____

_____

_____

_____

3. Enumerate (list) the aspects of your
   marriage that bring you joy. Why are these
   elements essential for the well-being of
   your marriage?

_____

_____

_____

_____

_____

_____

4. Compile a list of five qualities or actions
   about your spouse that you value and
   appreciate. How can you demonstrate

your appreciation for your spouse's uniqueness and significance in your life?

_____

_____

_____

_____

_____

_____

5. Engage in open communication with your spouse about these aspects. Practice communicating with your spouse rather than talking at them. Make a conscious effort to alter the way you express yourself to your spouse. Instead of resorting to accusations, practice active listening and empathy. Commit to understanding each other's perspectives and working towards resolutions rather than allowing conflicts to escalate. Reflect on the outcomes of this approach. How does this communication method resonate with you?

_____

_____

_____

_____

_____

_____

_____

_____

_____

_____

Prayer

Heavenly Father, *thank you for the fresh Breath of Your Holy Spirit that revitalizes me with life. Forgive me for my sins. Help me to submit to the guidance of Your Holy Spirit that I may be transformed into the best me that you have willed me to be. As I reflect upon myself and my marriage, I realize that decaying spirits of division and strife have riddled my relationship with myself as well as my husband/wife. Contentious spirits threatened to dissolve my marriage in divorce. Father, I turn to You seeking Your guidance. Help me to release the bitterness that has enveloped my spirit. Help me to release the toxins that have poisoned my soul. Touch the heart of my* *marriage, Father. Touch my eyes as well as the eyes of my husband/wife that we may see our way on this path of healing. Where there is bitterness, please allow us to drink from the sweet hydrating fountain of Your Holy Spirit. Help us to receive Your Wisdom. Stand with us, Father, as we travel this road of redemption for ourselves as well as our marriage. May our home be blessed and warmed by the luminating light of Your Holy Word. In the name of Yeshua, I pray. Amen.*

Chapter Ten
Sewing Fig Leaves
Hiding Behind The Shame

"Then the eyes of both of them were opened, and they realized they were naked; so they sewed fig leaves together and made coverings for themselves. 8) Then the man and his wife heard the sound of the Lord God as he was walking in the garden in the cool of the day, and they hid from the Lord God among the trees of the garden. 9) But the Lord God called to the man, "Where are you?" 10) He answered, "I heard you in the garden, and I was afraid because I was naked, so I hid." 11) And he said, "Who told you that you were naked? Have you eaten from the tree that I commanded you not to eat from?"
-- Genesis 3:7-11 NIV

Once you've tasted the forbidden, your eyes are opened to where you stand, often realizing it's not where you intended to be. Whether seeking excitement or breaking monotony, indulging in the forbidden - be it extramarital affairs or anything posing a threat to your marriage's sanctity - brings a stark realization of "nakedness." Did guilt follow, or did you revel in pleasure? Regardless, tasting the forbidden unveils where you've breached covenant, be it physically, emotionally, or spiritually.

The serpent omitted the consequences from Eve, that tasting the forbidden would awaken unknown desires and lead to destructive paths. Beyond the forbidden, Adam and Eve's marriage was irreversibly altered. They faced toil and pain, and jealousy led to murder in subsequent generations, sowing seeds of discord.

We hastily sew fig leaves to conceal our shame, hoping to hide imperfections from God, who sees all. Despite His omniscience, God beckons us, questioning, "Where are you?" not out of ignorance but to prompt us to acknowledge our fall. We live in brokenness, blaming others instead of accepting accountability for growth and healing.

Key Words:

shame, blame, accountability, hidden areas of bitterness and fault

Reflection Questions:
1. In what way(s) have you and/or your spouse tried to cover your marital mistakes with "fig leaves"?

_____

_____

_____

_____

_____

_____

2. How has shame hindered your marriage
   from moving forward into healing?
   Explain.

_____

_____

_____

_____

_____

_____

3. List three areas of bitterness/fault that
   make it difficult for your marriage to heal.
   Explain.

_____

_____

_____

_____

_____

_____

Healing The Break:

When couples engage in the "blame game," their marriage is undoubtedly in significant trouble. To initiate healing, it's crucial for both partners to approach the situation as mature adults, prioritizing healing over assigning blame. Sometimes, seeking marital counseling is necessary for this healing journey. Agree with your spouse to pursue counseling to address critical areas of need, as "fig leaves" cannot conceal mistakes.

- One major thing that has caused significant hurt within your marriage is:

_____

_____

_____

_____

_____

_____

- In what ways did you try to conceal your contribution to the hurt?

_____

_____

_____

_____

_____

- Have an open conversation with your spouse about being transparent regarding your faults.

- Forgive yourself for contributing to the hurt within the marriage.

- Request forgiveness from your spouse. Be specific about the pain you caused in the marriage.

- Commit to collaborating with your spouse to address and heal the hidden areas of ugliness within your marriage.

Prayer

Jehovah Raphe, *the Lord my healer! I come to you thanking you for opening my eyes to the areas of weaknesses and pain within my marriage. Father, I come to you humbly yielding the pain of my marriage. Jehovah Adonai, my Lord, I come submitting the cares of my marriage unto your Almighty Hands. Into your Holy Hands, Father, I lay my faults and contributions to the hurt, pain, and discord that I have birth into my marriage. Forgive me, Father, for any deception and violation that I have committed against you and against my marriage. Forgive me, Father, for disrespecting my husband/wife by entertaining and having conversations with serpents. Father, help me to not leave my husband/wife alone within this marriage. May my husband/wife and I be as wise as the cunning serpent but harmless as doves that we know how he operates yet take authority over his schemes and lies. May my husband/wife and I be filled with your Holy Spirit and guided by Your Light. Through the authority of your Holy Word, Father, my husband/wife and I are more than conquerors over any scheme, tactic, plan, or strategy that Satan devises to destroy our marriage. My husband/wife and I are one through your Holy Spirit. We plead the Blood of Yeshua over and upon our marriage. We are healed through the Blood of your precious Lamb. Our marriage is healed and made whole through the Blood of Jesus Christ. My husband/wife and I will no longer "sew fig leaves" to hide our weaknesses and faults. We come to You, Father, because you light our path. Through You, Father, we will eat of the fruit of Your Spirit; thereby we will be fruitful and multiply as* *you have commanded us. We will not miscarry or abort any seed that you have planted in us. We will birth everything that you have deposited within us. In the Name of Yeshua we pray. We honor Your Name and we magnify You. Thank you, Father. Amen.*

Scriptural Meditations:

*I would seek unto God, and unto God would I commit my cause. **Job 5:8***

Question: What are three specific things you desire in your marriage? How will you commit these things to God to help integrate them into your marriage?

_____

_____

_____

_____

_____

_____

*Thou shalt also decree a thing and it shall be established unto thee; and the light shall shine upon thy ways. **Job 22:28***

Question: What are three specific things you decree in your marriage and your home? Find three scriptures to guide you in those things. Declare them over yourself, your marriage, and your home.

_____

_____

_____

_____

_____

_____

> *All a man's ways are pure in his own eyes, but his motives are weighed out by the Lord.* **Proverbs 16:2**

Question: List three arguments that you feel justified concerning your spouse and your home. List your motives in each. Are they helpful to support only you? Do they consider not just you but your spouse and your home? Explain.

_____

_____

_____

_____

_____

_____

> *Commit your way to the Lord? Trust in Him and He will do it* **Psalm 37:5**

Question: List three things you would like to improve on. Declare Psalm 37: 5 over your life. Note your progress as you declare this scripture over your life and submit to the Lord.

_____

_____

_____

_____

_____

_____

> *Cast your burden upon the LORD and He will sustain you; He will never let the righteous be shaken.* **Psalm 55:22**

Question: What is one burden you and your spouse

are carrying in your marriage? Declare Psalm 55:22 over your marriage. Communicate with one another. Commit to change as you cast that burden unto God's Authority. Seek counseling for further support.

_____

_____

_____

_____

_____

_____

> *In all your ways acknowledge Him, and He will make your paths straight.* **Proverbs 3:6**

Question: Do you acknowledge habits and faults that are not helpful in your marriage? Admit those habits and faults to God, your spouse, your home. Commit to changing habits that will better serve you, your marriage, and your home. Declare Proverbs 3:6 daily upon your life.

_____

_____

_____

_____

Prayer

May your marriage be transformed as you renew your mind to the Word of God. May God's Presence and Power manifest and be the Authority within your home and marriage. I speak life and healing to you, your home, your marriage. May you flourish and walk in the Spirit of God. Blessings, healing, and peace unto you my brothers and sisters as you grow and prosper abundantly in Christ. Thank God. Amen.

Thank You for Reading!

Other Books by Prophetess Sherri Thomas

Healing Springs: Claim the Healing Within

COMING SOON

The second book in the Broken Rib Series:

The Glass House:
Looking Through a Rose-Colored Glass

The third book in the Broken Rib Series:

The Glass House:
Shattered Walls-Shattered Foundation

The fourth book in the Broken Rib Series:

The Glass House:
Forged by Fire- The Darkstone Legacy

Contact:

If this book has blessed you, send me an email and/or visit my website to let me know. I look forward to hearing from you. You may also log onto my website for the latest updates from the author.

Website: https://sheesoars.com/
Email: SherriT@gmail.com -- Blessings!

Made in the USA
Columbia, SC
25 May 2024

35715277R00052